# HOW TO CHOOSE

# &

I0474098

# WORK WITH AN

# ATTORNEY!!!

*Increase Your Chances of Winning*
*and*
*Decrease Your Legal Fees!!!*

Save Money, Time & Your Sanity!!

By: Art Lorentzen

ISBN-13: 978-1467910996
ISBN-10: 1467910996

# Disclaimer

The information contained in this book is intended to be educational and not for legal advice whatsoever. The author is not an attorney. This information should not replace consultation with a competent attorney. The content of the book is intended to be used as an adjunct to a rational and responsible legal program prescribed by an attorney. The author and publisher are in no way liable for any misuse of the material.

# TABLE OF CONTENTS

# Introduction

After being name a Defendant in a lawsuit, you are left with only two choices: 1.) represent yourself or 2.) hire an attorney to represent you. The cruel hard fact is that most people have no choice, but to hire an attorney. ***This book will help you "INCREASE YOUR CHANCES OF WINNING, WAYS TO CONCLUDE THE LAWSUIT QUICKER WHILE DECREASING YOUR LEGAL FEES".*** You will receive incite on the inner workings of a lawsuit from the perspective of a Defendant - information that you will not receive from an attorney.

While your choices are limited, a Plaintiff has many more choices, the best of which is whether to proceed with the lawsuit or not. Finding the right attorney at a reasonable price that is also someone you are comfortable with is very important. Therefore this informational book is written from the prospective of the Defendant. Once named as a Defendant, you will have no alternative but to defend yourself. If you do not, you will lose and a default judgment will be entered against you.

The book will take you step by step through the process of choosing and working with an attorney. Hiring an attorney is an expensive proposition, which can get quickly out of hand.

**The bottomline to this book is to provide you information that will assist you in choosing and working with the right attorney thus increasing your chances of winning the lawsuit, ways to conclude the lawsuit quicker while keeping your legal fees down. You do not want to let the legal fees drain you of all your financial resources, possibly resulting in your personal and/or your company's bankruptcy. Because if that were to happen you will have to represent yourself, which increases your**

chances of losing, and possibly lose a lawsuit you should win.

**NEVER DISCOUNT YOUR OWN ABILITY TO UNDERSTAND AND MANAGE YOUR LAWSUIT.**

The author of this informational book is not an attorney and the book does not give legal advice, but offers the reader incite into the workings of a lawsuit based upon the author's own personal experience. The book is written in understandable plain English for the layperson.

# CHAPTER I

# You Have Been Named a Defendant in a Lawsuit

You have just been named as a Defendant in a Lawsuit, which leaves you with no alternative but to defend yourself. If you do not, a default judgment will be entered against you. When you receive the summons naming you as a Defendant in a lawsuit, you will get a sick feeling in your stomach. You will be angry, but you have to deal with the problem.

Unfortunately the legal system does not have a review process to weed out malicious, abusive and frivolous lawsuits in order that the lawsuit can be immediately dismissed before you have to hire an attorney. The legal system forces you to hire an attorney to prove to the court that the lawsuit has no merit, instead of the Plaintiff having to prove to the court or a panel for the court that his/her case has merit. In any case, you will have to defend yourself regardless of how you feel about the validity and merits of the lawsuit.

# CHAPTER II
# Where Do You Find an Attorney?

Finding an attorney can be a cumbersome and difficult task, but is necessary. If you are sued in a State that you do not reside in, you will have to engage/hire an attorney in that State. Out of State lawsuits are more difficult to manage, but it can be done.

There are three main places to find attorneys. One is a recommendation/referral, second in the Yellow Pages (because it lists attorneys local to the state that you are sued in) and the third is Martindale Hubbell's (www.martindale.com) attorney directory. Everyone is probably familiar with the Yellow Pages, but not Martindale Hubbell. Martindale Hubbell lists law firms and his/her attorneys as well as individual attorneys. Here you can find the legal specialty(s) you are looking for. Martindale Hubbell rates every attorney, which can assist you in weeding out the good from the mediocre. All three sources compliment each other.

The lawsuit lists causes or claims against you. From these you can determine the legal specialty(s) that your chosen attorney will need. Next you can look in the Yellow Pages for an attorney that will meet your specific legal needs. Make a list, which will include large firms, small firms and one or two attorney firms.

Take the list and either go to Martindale Hubbell's website or view the books at the local university/college law library, if one is nearby. Begin by looking up the law firms first and then review the information provided. Read the biographies on the partners and the attorneys. See what the ratings are. The law firms' website may be listed, but if it is not you can perform a google search to find it. The website generally lists the attorneys and his/her area of expertise. Then do the same for the small firms and the one or two attorney firms. Make notes as you go along, highlighting those you wish to talk to.

# CHAPTER III

# Initial Contact with Attorneys

You now have made a list of attorneys to contact. On that list it is a good idea to have attorneys from the large, small and one to two attorney firms. When you start making your phone calls, you should have the following along side of you:

1.) a copy of the compliant/cause;

2.) basic information highlighting the people involved;

3.) background information (what lead up to the lawsuit);

4.) brief answers addressing each claim/count in the compliant/cause; and

5.) list of your questions you want to ask the attorney.

Attorneys do not have much time to spare, so you want to be concise, orderly and as efficient as you can be on the telephone. You will eventually fax, email or mail the above information to the attorneys you are interested in. Please note: not every attorney will be interested in your case and you will not be interested in each attorney you speak with. There are a variety of reasons for this, but usually comes down to fees, personality and availability.

During these initial calls be sure to discuss his/her hourly rate, not only the attorney you are talking to, but the rates of junior attorneys who most likely will perform much of the work on the lawsuit, paralegals and legal technicians. Discuss retainer and how it will be used. Discuss some less mundane costs such as faxing, research, and copying. Discuss how they calculate his/her hours i.e. travel time. Last but not least will they provide a budget and will monthly invoices be detailed and billed on time.

At this point, you send (fax, email or mail) the information you have put together to your short list of attorneys (5 or 6). You will eventually choose an attorney from this group. Feedback from these attorneys will be in the form of a telephone call, meeting or a letter. Take notes of all telephone calls and meetings.

# CHAPTER IV

# Who Do You Choose?

All your telephone calls and/or meetings have been made; you have sent information and received feedback from the attorneys. **Who do you choose?**

Choosing an attorney will be a very important decision, so take your time, but do not linger on a decision. You will have legal documents to file and you want to get started. You will be living with your decision most likely throughout the entire lawsuit, as switching attorney's and law firms is not an easy and cheap task once you have gotten into the lawsuit.

You should consider the following quality and factors in an attorney and the law firm:

1.) Rate. Rate is continually stressed, because you do not want the legal fees to bankrupt you, resulting in you being unable to continue to hire an attorney. You will have to find your comfortable balance between rate and quality. The rates will vary by position in the law firm and not necessarily by experience. The following is a range of rates you can expect to pay:

a.) partner (highest level) - $350/hr to $500/hr

b.) associate attorney (2$^{nd}$ highest level) - $225/hr. to $350/hr.

c.) junior attorney (3$^{rd}$ highest level) - $160/hr. to $225/hr.

d.) legal assistant/technician - $90/hr. to $120/hr.

e.) paralegal – $95/hr. to $150/hr.

These rates will also vary by area of the country. The higher cost of living areas will naturally be more expensive than the lower cost of living areas.

2.)   Personality – easy to work with, but aggressive.  You want an aggressive attorney in order to resolve the lawsuit as quickly and efficiently as possible.

3.)   Expertise/knowledge in the area of your lawsuit.  How many years of experience?  How many defendant cases has the attorney litigated and make sure the attorney is a litigator.  Knows his/her way around a courtroom.

4.)   Attorney's support structure.  You want to know if the attorney has the support structure (paralegal, research, secretarial, copy) to get all the work done timely and efficiently.  This can be a two edged sword, in that a large support structure has lots of overhead and can be cumbersome, inefficient and expensive.

5.) Availability. You want to know that the attorney's current caseload is not already overloaded, which would cause your lawsuit to drag on.

6.) Will the Attorney let you be involved. You want the attorney to assure you that they will listen to your suggestions and ideas with the willingness to implement them. After all you are paying the bill and the attorney needs to follow your instructions. You do not want to just set back and let the attorney run off on his/her own. The lawsuit will have business issues as well as legal issues.

7.) The attorney's use of expert witness and other special outside aids. This is an area where costs can really get out of hand for little value. Be sure recommended expert witness(s) are needed and are expert in the field you need. For example, a forensic accountant who specializes in divorce lawsuits may not be a good choice in a business lawsuit. If your attorney wants to give a fancy presentation with outside visual aids, first see if it is absolutely necessary and second how much does it cost. Nothing is free. Sometimes being fancy is not the best, particularly if the presentation does not come off well i.e. equipment fails. In this instance, not only have you wasted thousands of dollars, but have probably hurt your chances of winning the lawsuit.

8.) Will the attorney prepare a budget. It is nice to have a budget, but rarely will an attorney prepare one even after they have promised one. The attorney does not want to be held accountable to numbers on a budget, especially when there can be overruns.

Using all the above information, you are now in a position to make an informed attorney selection that best suits your budget and your lawsuits needs. You should prioritize the factors in the order that is important to you. Remember, inefficiencies and rate can cause a lawsuit to drag on forever, beyond the normal drag on in a case, but you do not want to add to it. Unnecessary and lengthy delays (lawsuits can last 5 – 10 years) can cause you financial hardship and emotional distress to the point that winning and losing no longer matters.

# CHAPTER V

# What To Believe and Not Believe From Your Attorney?

Throughout the course of the lawsuit, your attorney will give you advice, direction and status concerning your lawsuit. This is needed; however, you have to make sure it all makes sense and is believable. In order for you to assess this information, you need a working knowledge of the law that fits the nature of your lawsuit. Just as you would do in other situations i.e. purchasing a computer, you would acquire a working knowledge of the specific features of the computer you are considering in order that you may talk intelligently with the salesperson.

You are not becoming an attorney, but in order to understand and evaluate what your attorney is telling you, you are going to need some basic understanding in the following areas:

1.) Who is the Judge? and the Judge's background

2.) Court procedures

3.) Jury vs. non-jury trial

4.) Court documents to be filed, filing time frames and their purpose i.e. interrogatories, request for documents, deposition, motion for summary judgment are some.

5.) Various legal terms (please refer to the Glossary for the more common terms)

6.) Lawsuit strategy and timeline, and

7.) Able to read and understand your legal bill

By knowing the above information you will be in a better position to understand and manage your lawsuit as well as communicate somewhat intelligently with your attorney. This information is knowledge and knowledge is everything. With knowledge will you be better able to determine what your attorney says makes sense or not.

Although your attorney is the expert, that does not make your attorney always correct and believable. First your attorney can make a mistake just as any one can; however, his/her mistakes can be costly with the chance of losing the lawsuit and extra legal fees. You will have to be able to recognize when a mistake is made and/or the strategy is flawed in order to protect yourself. Even though you expect your attorney to tell the truth that does not always happen. For instance, your attorney may give you a reason for a delay in filing papers or asked for an extension of time, but the real reason may be that your attorney just picked up another client that is more important to the law firm and your attorney is diverting his/her attention to this new client. Basically, you have been put on the back burner. Another instance may be that the attorney asks for an extension of time to file a court document. Your attorney tells you that the extension is a strategic maneuver when in fact your attorney forgot about filing the document that would cause the deadline to be missed. You will have to query your attorney as to how the extension is a strategic maneuver. His/her answer will help you determine whether the extension is legitimate or not. This is an example that causes further delays in the lawsuit and possibly leads to extra costs to you. Reasons given are not always the truth and hopefully you can recognize them.

You also need to go over the lawsuit strategy with your attorney in order that you both are on the same page. With a strategy it will be easier for you to monitor and follow your case.

If you stay involved and push your attorney, the lawsuit should move along. However, you need to strike a balance, in that the more telephone calls, emails and faxes you make, the larger your legal bill. Nothing is free.

# CHAPTER VI
# Your Involvement

Your involvement in the lawsuit is critical to reach your most favorable outcome. You will need to determine, independent of your attorney your most favorable outcome and as the lawsuit progresses you may need to revise it. Your most favorable outcome is emphazied, because what is a favorable outcome to you may not be the same favorable outcome to your attorney. A win does not mean you are both happy with the outcome, particularly if it is a settlement that you are advised to take, although you may not agree with it. Also, sometimes a loss is the same as a win to an attorney, if they feel the financial loss is not that bad in his/her eyes. However, the loss may seem a lot in yours. Simply put, you both do not share the same stake.

In order to bring your attorney and your outcome views closer, your involvement is crucial. If you do not get involved and/or are not knowledgeable about the legal proceedings and your lawsuit, it will be easy for you to miss facts and not be able to intelligently discuss your lawsuit with your attorney.

The outcome to you can be a lasting affect on your life, your job, your family's life, your future and your wallet. The outcome to your attorney is just another job to them and when the lawsuit is over and the legal bills are paid, you will be forgotten. To minimize this gap your involvement from day one is necessary.

The knowledge you acquire in Chapter VI will assist you with your involvement. Your involvement will also keep your attorney on his/her toes, knowing that they cannot snow you and you are holding them accountable on all aspects of your lawsuit. You will want to participate in the overall lawsuit strategy, timeline, court documents to be filed, settlement strategy, explanation of documents produced by you and Plaintiff, development of interrogatory questions, request for documents, and the review of drafts of all court documents (provide input with particular emphasis on accuracy of the facts). Remember, your attorney is new to the issues surrounding the lawsuit and your input is valuable. What may seem as an insignificant, unintentional misinterpretation of a fact may become a critical issue to overcome later in the lawsuit. Your attorney will attempt to get up to speed with all the details, but you will always have more knowledge, simply because you were the one always involved from the beginning.

Your attorney will depend upon you to maintain the accuracy and correctness of the facts surrounding your lawsuit.

# CHAPTER VII
# Getting Started

Now you have reached the point where you need to get started. The first order of business for your attorney will be to answer the lawsuit denying any wrong doings. The first order of business for you is to gather all documents relating to the counts/claims stated against you in the lawsuit for the time period noted.

Answering the lawsuit is routine. Your gathering of the documents will be more cumbersome, frustrating, time consuming and expensive. If you have a lot of documents, you may want to consider purchasing a copy machine with an automatic feeder to copy yourself. This is probably the least expensive method of copying the documents. You are only out your time. The reason for this is that you will be giving all the original documents to your attorney and it is important for you to maintain at least one copy for your records. You want to maintain control over at least a copy and there will be times that you will have to refer to the documents. It is easier to refer to them when you have a copy.

An alternative, which is probably the second least expensive method is to pay to have the documents copied by the local office supply store, but you have to lug all the documents down to them; those working at the store will start to know your business (i.e. you have been sued, if this is an issue); and you lose control of the original documents.

The last alternative is to bring the original documents to your attorney's office for copying. This will be extremely expensive. You be paying a large price per copy plus an hourly rate of the person making the copies.

Buying an $800 - $1,000 copy machine in the end will be the most efficient, controlled and least expensive way.

Please note: do not begin copying your documents until you receive a formal request for documents. That request will specifically list the documents the Plaintiff is seeking and those are the only documents at that time that you will need to produce. You only want to produce the documents requested. Also, there is no need to produce multiple copies of the exact same document. Doing so will only add to your cost of copying and the cost charged by your attorney to copy the originals, to put them in order and place the Bates Numbering (numbering system) on each page. The cost of bates numbering and organizing each document by your attorney's paralegal or legal technician can be in the thousands of dollars.

While you are gathering, not copying, your documents, your attorney should begin to prepare for submission to the Plaintiff a list of interrogatories (questions) and a request for documents. At the same time the Plaintiff will probably make the same requests through your attorney. Once the request(s) has been received you can begin to organize your original documents by request number and then begin copying the original documents. Once copied bring them over to your attorney who will then have his support staff prepare them to answer the request for documents. Your attorney will at this point bates numbering each page of each document and then make two copies: one copy to answer the Plaintiff's request for documents and one for your attorney's records. Your attorney will retain the originals.

The above request for documents by themselves (Defendant and Plaintiff) can take months to complete, but this is how you will get started.

You will submit answers to the interrogatories to your attorney who probably revise them to be more precise and shorter.

# CHAPTER VIII
## What is next?

At this point the Plaintiff and you (Defendant) have exchanged your Request for Documents (there may be multiple requests) and Interrogatories (there may be multiple requests). You have copied your documents and answered the Plaintiff's questions.

Your goal at this point is to gather sufficient facts to file your "Motion for Summary Judgment" with the court. A Motion for Summary Judgment is a court document that asks the court to dismiss all charges and the lawsuit as a <u>matter of law</u> based upon documents produced, not on hearsay. It is always best to reference as many of the Plaintiffs documents, answers to interrogatories and depositions as possible, as they produced the information, thus they cannot dispute their authenticity. Your attorney will research case law (for the State the lawsuit is in or Federal law if in Federal court) to be cited (mentioned) in the Motion to support your request to have the charges and lawsuit dismissed as a <u>matter of law</u>. This Motion can be the quickest and least costly way out of the lawsuit. If the Motion is granted, the case is over and there is no trial. The Plaintiff will have the appeal process available to them. Further discussion of the Motion for Summary Judgment will be in Chapter XII – Legal Documents to File.

The next step is to review the documents your attorney has received from the Plaintiff through the Request for Production of Documents. Although your attorney will review this information, if you have time it is a good idea for you to perform your own independent review. Since it is not cost effective to have the documents copied, you will arrange a time with your attorney to reserve a small conference room for you to use for your review. The answers to the interrogatories generally are not that voluminous; therefore, they can be copied and sent to you for your review.

The reason these reviews are necessary is that you are the most knowledgeable about the circumstances surrounding your lawsuit. Your reviews will not only assist your attorney in gaining more knowledge of the particulars of your lawsuit, but to make sure important documents are not overlooked or viewed as not important. You need to provide your attorney with your written short and concise comments.

After these reviews your attorney and you will discuss depositions to be taken. A deposition is where attorneys ask questions one on one to some one of interest to them. The person whose deposition is being taken is under oath to provide truthful answers to the questions. A court recorder is there to record the questions and answers as well as any other discussions that are on the record. The deposition, in some instances may be video taped. Later the transcript and video of the deposition can be purchased, which is what your attorney will do.

Whose deposition do you take? The Plaintiff for sure, any one else from the Plaintiff's side that you feel has knowledge of some or all of the facts surrounding your lawsuit, and expert witnesses that the Plaintiff is providing. As far as expert witness goes, you want to find out what they have to say in order that your attorney can prepare a defense to the expert testimony.

Your attorney and you will review the deposition transcript(s) and videotape(s) once they become available. After all depositions have been reviewed, your attorney and you will discuss (over the phone seems to always be the most efficient and effective way for discussions) whether you have enough information to file your Motion for Summary Judgment. Your attorney will best be able to make this determination. Your knowledge of the inner workings of a Motion or Partial Motion for Summary Judgment will assist you in evaluating and understanding your attorney's recommendation.

If your attorney recommends that there is not enough information, then you may have to do another Request for Production of Documents, another set of Interrogatories, and/or a follow-up deposition or a deposition of someone else who arose from the depositions. Once your attorney feels you have all the necessary information and you agree, then the Motion or Partial Motion for Summary Judgment can be filed. A full Motion for Summary Judgment is the best court document to file, as it will get rid of the entire lawsuit at one time. A partial is just that, only part(s) of the lawsuit are dismissed.

Depending on the State the lawsuit is filed or if the lawsuit is Federal Court, the procedure (particularly time frame) for the Plaintiff to answer the Motion for Summary Judgment and your response, if allowed in the State, may be different. Also, it is a good idea that your attorney request a hearing before the Judge in order to provide the Judge with any additional facts (not hearsay or information that causes a dispute of the facts) and answer any questions the Judge may have. After this process, the Judge at his/her pace will rule on the Motion for Summary Judgment. This could take weeks or months, there is no set time frame imposed on the Judge to act. During this time the case is dormant.

The Judge now rules, if in your favor than the Plaintiff will most likely appeal to the governing appeals court. The appeal procedure will depend on the State and Federal courts. Generally, the process is the Plaintiff will file an appeal, the Defendant will answer and the Plaintiff may or may not be allowed to respond depending upon the rules of that State (in Federal Court the Plaintiff can respond). The appeals process, as far as filing the court documents and all the responses, can take at least 90 days, but most likely more, particularly if one of the parties asks for an extension of time. A hearing may or may not be set. The real lost time is waiting for the appeals court to act on the appeal either first by scheduling a hearing and then ruling or ruling without a hearing. This could take from 1 to 2 years for a final ruling.

If the Judge denies the Motion for Summary Judgment then the lawsuit will go to trial. Again, although you may think the legal process moves at a normal pace, it does not. Trial dates are often set 8 months to a year out from the date the court sets the date; however, the court may not get around to setting a date for months. Then often times the date is changed (another 8 months to a year out) for a variety reasons, such as the Defendant or Plaintiff is not ready or the court has had a change of schedule. A trial scheduled for February could be rescheduled to December. In any case, before the trial there will be trial preparation during which the court will require at least a Joint Pretrail Order.

This document can be very lengthy and costly to you.

For the trial, your attorney will line up witness(s) and experts depending if there are any. Lines of questioning will be discussed and actual questions will be written that will be asked by your attorney of each witness. Exhibits to be displayed at the trial will be selected and blown up or drawn on a flip chart.

A trial can be very expensive (running into the thousands of dollars and possibly tens of thousands) depending upon the following factors:

1.) Jury vs. non-jury trial. A jury trial takes longer because of jury selection (one to two days) and the constant need for the Judge to clarify issues and give jury instructions during the course of the trial and at the end of the trial preparing the jury instructions.

2.) The number of total witnesses and the time spent with each witness. Some witnesses may take only 2 – 3 hours where another witness may take 1 – 2 days. The time depends on the witnesses importance to the case. Plus each attorney will have the opportunity to ask questions with one attorney (the attorney who originally called the witness) has the opportunity for one rebuttal.

3.) The cooperativeness of the attorneys on both sides. If they are uncooperative and objecting to everything just for the sake of being a pain, the trial will get bogged down. As much as the Judge says they will move the trial along, they are somewhat reluctant to push and scold attorneys.

4.) Technical issues, Judge's schedule and interruptions. The Judge may take a longer lunch than most in order that they may act on other work before them.

5.)    Equipment rental, if any.

6.)    Next day trial preparation. At the end of each trial day your attorney will go back to his/her office and prepare for the next day based upon that days events. Sometimes this can be another 5 - 10 hours of legal fees per day plus possible support staff.

All the above items add to the amount of time it takes to complete the trial. And the delays during the trial day, may keep your attorney, expert witness(s) and you waiting around. For example, your expert witness was asked to arrive at 1:00pm to give testimony at 1:30pm, but the previous witness took longer and your expert did not go on until 3:30pm. You will pay for those 2 extra unplanned hours. You will pay your attorney and others his/her hourly fee while they sit around doing nothing.

At the conclusion of a jury trial you will have an outcome, but at a non-jury the judge most likely will not rule from the bench and you have to wait a few days for the outcome. In any case, the loser will have the right to appeal the decision.

# CHAPTER IX
# Legal Services

There are a number of legal services that you as an individual, non-attorney can avail yourself of. The type of legal service(s) you use will depend upon your involvement. At a minimum you should research the either the State or Federal laws (depends upon whether you are in State or Federal court) that will affect you lawsuit. For example, if a claim deals with trade secrets then you will want to research trade secret laws.

State and Federal laws are available on the internet. In fact, the internet is a terrific research tool. You can ask questions (make calls to State or Federal agency lawyers), look up information pertaining to the claims against you and other useful information.

There are more formal legal services available such as Westlaw; Fastcase, Inc. and the local university legal library. Learn how to conduct research on the internet. Most people already have a working knowledge in other areas that they just need to apply to a legal forum.

If you plan to do some or all of the case law legal research, you will need to use Westlaw or Fastcase or other similar services that are out there. You will need to learn how to conduct legal research. Most research services have attorneys on staff that can help you.

There is not much free legal advice available unless you meet certain low-income requirements. Therefore, you will have to do a lot of self-teaching through reading and understanding.

# CHAPTER X

# How to Keep the
# Legal Bills Low?

Receiving and paying your legal bills most likely be the most stressful part of your lawsuit. Oddly enough, your legal bills can bankrupt you long before a decision by the court has made. Even if you win the lawsuit, you may still be the loser, because of the legal bills. Therefore, it is with the utmost importance that you monitor and pay close attention as how your attorney spends your money.

Through the course of the lawsuit your attorney will know how much you make a year and will be able to determine your standing in the financial community.

Once your attorney realizes you have money, your attorney will try the utmost to get it from you. It will all be done in the name of giving you the best possible legal defense. Attorneys eyes light up when they know his/her client has lots of money. Please keep in mind that although your attorney is your friend/partner in the lawsuit, your attorney is also in business to make money. You can receive legal bills totaling $20,000 - $30,000 a month for what appears to be a simple defense. When you do receive a legal bill for $5,000 for a month, you will think you just hit the lottery.

So how do you keep the legal bills low and within reason? For one thing you have to make sure that your attorney does not overkill, that is your attorney does not research an issue to death, involve other attorneys to review your attorney's work, start and restart the same issue, too many attorneys attending meetings, depositions or hearings and excessive charging for research services. At the rate you pay your attorney you are entitled to expect your attorney to bring a certain degree of knowledge and experience to the table. Your attorney should not have to do extensive research when your attorney should already possess that knowledge. After all you hired your attorney and pay the high hourly rate for his/her experience and knowledge that they should already possess.

If you attorney is not efficient and drafts and redrafts of court documents are produced, your legal bill will increase. Your attorney has to account to the law firm for all his/her hours in a day and has to be a fee/income producer. This is particularly important if your attorney is in a large firm and wants to become a partner. Fee/income generators make partner, not the paper shuffler. Another area that can cause bills to increase, are delays in the lawsuit. For example, your attorney reviews the documents you provide and the documents and interrogatories submitted by the Plaintiff in one month, the lawsuit has a delay/lull in it and seven months later the lawsuit starts up again.  Your attorney will have forgotten what he/she read seven months ago and has to refresh his/her memory by rereading everything.  This is an instance where you pay for the same work twice.  Also, when lawsuits get stretched over years and they do, you run the risk of your attorney leaving the firm.  In this instance, you either follow him/her to the new firm if it is still in the same State or you will be assigned a new attorney who will have to get up to speed by reading everything that has already been read twice.  Now you are paying a third time for the same work.  For that reason, it is even more important that the lawsuit continue along a constant pace without lulls in the action that puts the lawsuit dormant for extended periods of time.  These are all ways how your legal bill can get out of hand and get out of hand in a hurry.

The following are ways to keep the bill reasonable although you may never think the bills are reasonable:

1.) Bills are sent to you monthly and on time. Sometimes bills are not sent every month and the next thing you know, you receive a bill for two months for $50,000 and you had no idea that this much work was going into the lawsuit.

2.) Bills are itemized by day, description of work, hours spent, who did the work and hourly rate.

3.) Review each line and make sure that the work was actually done for your lawsuit. Sometimes another client's work inadvertently ends up on your bill. Review for duplications, first: by mistake and second: because of inefficiencies.

4.) Excessive charges for services such as research service, copy, fax, telephone. Law firms contract for annual subscriptions to research services i.e.

Westlaw to research case law. The contract allows for unlimited use of the service. Also, this contract is just plain part of doing business, no different than the law firm paying rent for the space they occupy, the cost is already factored into the hourly rated. However, some law firms will charge you research services fees, although, they are not charged individually by use. These charges, which are separate from the hourly charge for the person actually performing the research, can run into the thousands of dollars. You should not be charged for this research service or at the least a normal amount. Remember, law firms are trying to pass as many of its costs as possible along to you. Watch for excessive copying charges in the form of cost per page and the actual number of pages copied. You do not want them to get carried away with too much copying.

5.) Watch for work that is nice to have, but not necessary. For instance, your attorney can spend a lot of time preparing an exotic timeline chart of your case history (will be looked at far less that time required to prepare) that is probably not necessary, where in the alternative just a simple list of case events is all that is required. Work such as this can run you thousands of dollars. After awhile a few thousand here and a few thousand there will add up to tens of thousands of dollars.

Another example is in the instance after you have had your lawsuit dismissed and your attorney recommends that you file a court document to recover your legal fees and costs from the Plaintiff. On the surface it appears to be the right action to take; however, you really need to take a look at the current financial situation of the Plaintiff. If the Plaintiff does not have the money to pay your legal fees and costs (you will get a feel for the Plaintiff's financial condition during the course of the lawsuit), then it does not make any sense to file those court documents. The cost of preparing the court document, which includes a detailed listing of your legal fees and costs, may be more and significantly more than the amount money you will probably collect. Also, keep in mind Judges are reluctant to make the Plaintiff pay all your legal fees and costs, therefore, the amount you will be awarded (collecting is another issue) will be a small percentage of what you had asked for. Another instance of where you win the battle, but lose the war.

6.) Poor case management by your attorney can result in the court requiring court documents that would not have been necessary if your attorney had managed/planned the timing of your lawsuit correctly. A good example of this is in the instance where your attorney has let the lawsuit linger and the court sets a trial date. What happens here is that by the time your attorney gathers the information to file your Motion for Summary Judgment, then actually files your Motion for Summary Judgment plus all the replies going back forth that Plaintiff and

Defendant are entitled to and there has not been a decision by the court on your Motion for Summary Judgment, you are now bumping up against the trial date. In this scenario, the court will require the Plaintiff and the Defendant to file a Joint Pretrail Order a short period before the trial date. This is an extensive document that can cost you tens of thousands of dollars in legal fees and the document may never be used, because the Judge acted favorably on your Motion for Summary Judgment just before the trial. Your attorney will justify the costs by arguing that the court required the document, but the fact remains that if your attorney had planned properly then this document will have only been prepared after your Motion for Summary Judgment had been denied and you are now going to trial. You certainly do not want to pay for the preparation of a court document that you are not sure will be needed. You want to pay when you know for sure it is needed.

Finally, you want to stress with your attorney that you want to be frugal, not too fancy, plan ahead and not last minute, efficient, concise, not wasteful, no excessive delays and do not be the cause of any delays, and no filing of unnecessary court documents. Simply put you do not want to be wasteful and spend money recklessly.

# CHAPTER XI

# Legal Documents to File

There will be a number of legal (court) documents that your attorney will file on your behalf during the course of the lawsuit. Some will be simple and some will be complicated, but the content of them will be common sense, but penned in a legal terms and structure.

The more common court documents that will be filed by you as Defendant are listed below. Please note some of these documents could be filed more than once. The actual court document name may be different than the name listed below because of State and Federal differences. Also, the list does not include the names of documents that may be filed by the Plaintiff. Those documents will have to be reviewed by your Attorney and most likely have written responses filed with the court. Some of those documents will be the same as Defendants.

1.) Notice of Appearance (notification of the law firm representing you)

2.) Original Answer

3.) Joint Notice of Removal (this is if you want to remove the lawsuit to Federal Court)

4.) Notice of Filing Notice of Removal

5.) Motion to Transfer Venue to the District Court of <u>Name a State</u> (used to transfer to Federal Court in another State)

6.) Response to Plaintiff's Motion to Remand and Brief in Support (this is your response to the Plaintiff requesting that the lawsuit be sent back to the State court)

7.) Reply to Plaintiff's Response to Defendant's Joint Motion to Transfer

Venue to the District Court of <u>Name of State</u> and Brief in Support

8.) Substitution of Attorney (will be used if you change law firms – Notice of Appearance can also be used)

9.) Joint Interim Status Report (describes the current status of the lawsuit)

10.) Request for Production of Documents (could be multiple requests)

11.) Interrogatories (could be multiple requests)

12.) Notice of Intention to Take the Oral Deposition of <u>Name of Defendant</u>

13.) Response to Plaintiff's Request for Production of Documents (could be multiple responses depending on the number requests by Plaintiff)

14.) Answers to Interrogatories (could be multiple answers depending on the number of interrogatory documents sent by Plaintiff)

15.) Motion for Summary Judgment

16.) Reply to Plaintiff's Opposition to Motion for Summary for Summary Judgment

17.) Joint Pretrial Order (used to notify the court and the parties to the lawsuit of the exhibits to be used at the trial, if there is one)

18.) Motion for Attorney's Fees and Costs (only filed if you win and is cost effective)

19.) Opposition to Plaintiffs Notice of Appeal

20.) Various court documents to grant various extensions, change trial dates, responses to Plaintiff's court documents

As can be seen there are a number of regular court documents that will be filed. In addition there will most likely be more court documents filed, because of special circumstances surrounding your lawsuit and gamesmanship on the part of the attorneys from both sides.

# CHAPTER XII
# Continue Defending The Lawsuit vs. Settlement

A very important decision you face as your lawsuit progresses is to decide whether to continue defending the lawsuit or settle regardless if you are innocent or not. **Please note**: Settlement talks and proposals can be made at any time during the lawsuit. If you feel you will lose the lawsuit, then trying to settle is an easy decision to make. If you feel you are innocent, then deciding to settle the lawsuit is not an easy decision. In the later you have to put your personal feeling and pride aside to make a good business, money decision. Lots of times lawsuits are filed with the sole purpose of trying to extract money from the Defendant without going to trial. Figuring that the Defendant will settle rather than pay legal fees. In this instance the Plaintiff knows you have to hire an attorney and pay their legal fees.

If you are not innocent, then you have to figure out how much money you will likely have to pay and try to settle at some number significantly less. It is easier and cost effective to settle a lawsuit earlier on than waiting later. The reason is the legal fees are mounting on the Plaintiff's side that increases his/her settlement number plus cooperativeness between opposing attorneys may decrease. In addition, the longer you wait the costlier it is for you on your side of the table. You will be incurring more legal fees the longer you wait.

If you feel you are innocent, then you have to determine your cost of the lawsuit (legal fees, out of pocket expenses) verses a settlement number. You will want to settle if the settlement number is significantly less than your estimated cost of the lawsuit or a number you are comfortable with. Again the sooner you settle the lower the settlement number.

Settlements should always be the cheaper way out of the lawsuit. However, many times the sides are so far apart in their numbers and/or just plain uncooperative with each other and/or the Plaintiff brought the suit as a means of revenge (it is illegal to bring a lawsuit for revenge, but it is done). In the case of revenge, the Plaintiff is using the legal system as his/her aide in extracting money from the Defendant.

Settlements can be hard to come by.

# CHAPTER XIII
# Conclusion

Being a Defendant in a lawsuit is not a pleasant experience, but you as a Defendant have no choice but to defend yourself either by hiring an attorney or representing yourself (pro se). Hopefully, this book has given you information that you can use in your defense and to not only protect yourself from the Plaintiff, but oddly enough from your own attorney's fees. You certainly do not want to run out of money, before the lawsuit has reached a final decision. If you do, then you will have to take over your defense yourself, which will increase your chances of losing.

You can always borrow to the hilt, but at what cost do you continue to pay an attorney instead of taking over the defense yourself.

Otherwise, you could find yourself filing bankruptcy at the end.

By reading and following the information in this guide, you should limit the pitfalls that are waiting for you. You should be able to manage your lawsuit efficiently and effectively at the lowest cost possible. You will be able to determine what work is necessary, duplicative, unnecessary, strategy that is sound, a lawsuit that moves along and not linger, and you will not be agreeing to things without personal knowledge.

You will be at the top of your game, which will keep your attorney at the top of his/her game.

Best of Luck in your lawsuit!!!!

- THE END –

# GLOSSARY OF TERMS

The following glossary of terms is from: *Wikipedia: The Free Encyclopedia*. Wikimedia Foundation Inc. Updated 14 October 2003, 13:19 UTC. Encyclopedia on-line. Available from http://en.wikipedia.org/wiki/List_of_legal_terms. Internet. Retrieved 28 February 2007.

**Affidavit**

Written statement of fact, signed and sworn to before a person having authority to administer an oath.

**Answer**

In the common law, an answer is the first pleading by a defendant, usually filed and served upon the plaintiff within a certain strict time limit after a civil compliant or criminal information or indictment has been served upon the defendant. It may have been preceded by an *optional* "pre-answer" motion to dismiss or demurrer; if such a motion is unsuccessful, the defendant *must* file an answer to the compliant or risk an adverse default judgment.

The *answer* established which allegations (cause of action in civil matters) ser forth by the complaining party will be contested by the defendant, and states all the defendant's defenses, thus establishing the nature and parameters of the controversy to be decided by the court.

**Appeal**

Process by which a case is brought from one court to a higher court for review.

**Appellant**

The appellant in a new case (an appeal) can be either the claimant, defendant or respondent from the lower case, depending on who was the losing party. The winning party from the lower court, however, is now the *respondent.*

**Bates numbering (or Bates Stamping)**

Is used in the legal and business fields to sequentially number or date/time-mark images or documents as they are scanned or processed (for example, marking exhibits during the discovery stage of preparations for trial or identifying business receipts). This process provides identification, protection, and auto-increment numbering of the images.

Bates numbering is an organizational method mainly used to identify legal documents. During the discovery phase of litigation, there may be a large number of documents so the Bates number, named after the Bates automatic numbering machine, assigns an arbitrary unique identifier for each document. It is usually numeric, though it could be alphanumeric, too. The number is unique to the documents disclosed or produced in a case, but there is no standardized algorithm for determining this number.

## Change of Venue

A change of venue is a legal term that means that a case before a court will be heard in another jurisdiction versus the one where the said crime took place. This is done when there is a reason to think that a defendant will not receive a fair trial, for whatever the reason.

## Civil Law

In the common law, civil law refers to the area of law involving relations between private individuals as well as between people and organisations, which through incorporation, take on the legal status of individuals. Civil law, in this sense, is usually referring to in comparison to criminal law, which is that body of law involving the state against individuals (including incorporated organisations).

**Civil Procedure**
>Is the body of law that sets out the process that courts will follow when hearing cases of a civil nature (a "civil action", as opposed to a criminal action). These rules govern how a lawsuit or case may be commenced, what kind of service of process is required, the types of pleadings or statements of case, motions or applications, and orders allowed in civil cases, the timing and manner of depositions and discovery or disclosure, the conduct of trials, the process for judgment, various available remedies, and how the courts and clerks must function.

**Complaint**
>Is a formal legal document that sets out the basic facts and legal reasons (see: cause of action) that the filing party (the plaintiffs) believes are sufficient to support a claim against another person, persons, entity or entities (the defendants) that entitles the plaintiff(s) to a remedy (either money damages or injunctive relief).

**Court of Appeals**
>or (and in some American states) Court of Appeal is the title of a court which has the power to consider or hear an appeal. A court of appeal is also a superior court. In a

state, it is usually called the state supreme court.

## Cross Examination

Questioning of a witness during a trial or during the taking of a deposition, by the party opposed to the one who produced the witness.

## Default Judgment

Is a binding judgment in favor of the plaintiff when the defendant has not responded to a summons or has failed to appear before a court.

In a civil trial involving damages, a default judgment will enter the amount of damages pled in the original compliant. If proof of damages is required, the court may schedule another hearing on that issue.

A defendant can have a default judgment vacated, or set aside, by filing a motion, after the judgment is entered, by showing of a proper excuse.

## Defendant

Is any party who is required to answer the compliant of a plaintiff in a civil lawsuit before a court.

**Deposition**

Testimony taken under oath and recorded in an authorized place outside the courtroom.

**Discovery**

In law, discovery is the pre-trial phase in a lawsuit in which each party through the law of civil procedure can request documents and other evidence from other parties or can compel the production of evidence by using a subpoena or through other discovery devices, such as requests for production and depositions.

**Dismissal**

Termination of a legal proceeding prior to finding. A dismissal can be with or without prejudice.

**Direct Appeal**

A proceeding in which a convicted person asks a higher court to overturn a conviction or sentence received at the trial court based on alleged errors which appear in the trial record.

**Direct Examination**

Questioning of a witness in a trial, or at the taking of a deposition, by the party for whom the witness is testifying.

**Evidence**

The law of evidence governs the use of testimony (e.g. oral or written statements, such as an affidavit) and exhibits (e.g. physical objects) or other documentary material which is admissible (i.e. allowed to be considered by the trier of fact, such as jury) in a judicial or administrative proceeding (e.g., a court of law).

**Exhibit**

The paper, document, or other physical object received by the court as evidence during a trial.

**Federal Court**

The United State federal courts are the system of court's organized under the Constitution and laws of the federal government of the United States.

**Inadmissible**

That which under the established rules of evidence, cannot be admitted or received in court.

**Injunction**

Any court order prohibiting some parties from specific actions and/or activities (for example, working for a competitor in breach of duty to an existing employer) on penalty of contempt of court.  It is, in exceptional cases, possible to obtain a mandatory injunction, which is a court order compelling a certain course of action (for example, demolition of an illegal structure) on penalty of contempt of court.

## Inter Alia

"Among other things."  Used in pleadings before a court or opinions of a court. ie. "The defendant claims, inter alia, that the plaintiff fails to establish . . ."

## Interrogatories

(also know as Requests for Further Information) are a formal set of written questions propounded by one litigant and required to be answered by an adversary, in order to clarify matters of evidence and help to determine in advance what facts will be presented at any trial in the case.

## Judgment

In a legal context, is synonymous with the formal decision made by a court following a lawsuit.  At the same time the court may also make a range of court orders, such as imposing a sentence upon a guilty defendant in a criminal matter, or providing a remedy for the plaintiff in a civil matter.

In the United States, under the rules of civil procedures governing practice in federal courts and most state courts, the *entry of judgment* is the final order entered by the court in the case, leaving no further action to be taken by the court with respect to the issues contested by the parties to the lawsuit. With certain exceptions, only a *final judgment* is subject to appeal.

**Jurisdiction**

(from the Latin *ius, iuris* meaning "law" and *dicere* meaning "to speak") is the practical authority granted to a formally constituted legal body or to a political leader to deal with and make pronouncements on legal matters and, by implication, to administer justice within a defined area of responsibility.

**Jurisprudence**

Theory and philosophy of law, which determines appropriate goals and methods of justice.

**Judgment proof**

Used in tort law contexts to refer to defendants or potential defendants who are financially insolvent. Even if a plaintiff were to secure a legal judgment against an insolvent defendant, the defendant's lack of funds would make the satisfaction of that judgment difficult, if not impossible, to secure.

## Laches

An equitable defence accusing an opposing party of having "sat on its right"; as a result of this delay, the delaying party is underserving of equitable relief. It is a form of estoppel for delay.

## Lawsuit

Is a civil action brought before a court in which the party commencing the action, the plaintiff, seeks a legal remedy. Often, one or more defendants are required to answer the plaintiff's complaint.

## Legal Remedy

Is the means by which a court of law, usually in the exercise of civil law jurisdiction, enforces a right, imposes a penalty, or makes some other court order to impose its will.

## Libel

An untrue statement published in print and communicated to a third party with the purpose to damage the reputation of another.

### *Mareva* injunction

A remedy granted by a court to stop a defendant from dissipating its assets from beyond the court's jurisdiction, so as to frustrate judgment. It is named for the *Mareva* case, although it first appeared in the *Nippon* case.

### Mistrial

Erroneous or invalid trial. Usually declared because of prejudicial error in the proceedings, hung jury, or when the proceedings must be interrupted.

### Motions

Oral or writtne requests made by a party to an action and brought before a judge prior to, during, or after a trial.

### Objection

Statement by an attorney in opposition to testimony, or the attempted admission of evidence, and opposing its consideration as evidence.

### Offence

Any accusation of violation of law, whether it is a criminal violation (such as murder) or a non-criminal infraction (such as a parking ticket).

**On the merits**

Describes the ultimate decision or judgment of a case. A decision *on the merits* is a judgement based on the facts, rendered after a full presentation of the evidence has been heard, as opposed to one based on legal technicalities or procedure deficiencies.

**Petitioner**

Used in place of Plaintiff in simplified procedures, often called proceedings.

**Plaintiff**

Also known as a claimant or complainant, is the party who initiates a lawsuit (also known as an *action)* before a court. By doing so, the plaintiff seeks a legal remedy, and if successful, the court will issue judgment in favour of the plaintiff and make the appropriate court order (eg. an order for damages).

**Pleading**

In the law, is one of the papers filed with a court in a civil action, such as a complaint, a demurrer, or an answer. A *complaint* is the first pleading filed by a plaintiff which initiates a lawsuit. A complaint sets forth the relevant allegations of fact that give rise to one or more legal causes of action along with a prayer for relief whereas a *demurrer* is a pleading filed by a defendant which challenges the legal sufficiency of a complaint and an *answer* is a pleading which admits or denies the specific allegations set forth in a complaint and constitutes a general appearance by a defendant. A defendant may also file a cross-complaint as well as bringing other parties into a case by the process of impleader.

## Precedent

Judical decision that serves as an example for how to rule in similar cases.

## Prejudice

The ability of a party whose case has been dismissed to refile it with the court, usually after overcoming the issue that led to its dismissal. If a case is dimissed *with prejudice* it may not be refiled; if it is dismissed *without prejudice,* the plaintiff (civil) or prosecutor (criminal) is permitted to refile if they so wish.

## *Prima facie*

Latin for "At first sight." Self-evident; obvious. A prima facie case is where the plaintiff presents enough evidence to win outright barring any defences or additional evidence presented by the defendant.

## Pro hac vice

"For this occasion", application by an out-of-state lawyer to represent his or her client. Since lawyers are licensed by each state independently they must ask for permission of the court to appear in matters before any other state courts. Permission is generally granted though the details can vary from one jurisdiction to another.

## Pro per, Pro se

"For self", refers to an individual who represents himself (or herself), without a lawyer, in a court proceeding.

## Res Ipsa Loquitur

Latin for "the thing speaks for itself". In Torts, it is the doctrine providing that, in some circumstances, the mere fact of an accident's occurrence raises an inference of negligence so as to establish a prima facie case.

## Respondent

Also known as an *appellee*, is the party to an appeal in which a lower court judgement is in its favour. The appellee's opponent on appeal is the appellant. The appellee is required to respond to the petition, oral arguments, and legal briefs of the appellant.

### Rule Nisi

An order from a superior court to show cause. That is, the rule is absolute unless one can "show cause" to otherwise. Same as Decree nisi.

### Sine die

Indefinitely; literally, "without a date". Use in relation to adjournments of the Court or of a particular case for an indefinite period.

### Sine qua non

Also meaning "But for", generally refers to the test used to establish *causation in fact*. If the result would not have occurred 'but for' the actions taken by the defendant, then there exist causation.

### Slander

The tort of making false oral statements damaging to another person's reputation; the oral form of defamation.

### State Court

In the United States, a state court has jurisdiction over disputes with some connection to a U.S. state. Cases are heard before and evidence is presented in a trial court, which is usually located in a courthouse in the county seat.

### Subpoena

Coming from the Latin for "under penalty" (*sub poena*), a subpoena is a court process used to cause a witness to appear and give testimony, commanding him or her to appear before the court or magistrate therein named, at a time therein mentioned, to testify for the party named, under a penalty therein mentioned. This is formally called a subpoena *ad testificandum*, to differentiate from a subpoena *duces tecum*, which refers to documents.

On proof of service of a subpoena upon the witness, and that he is material, a citation may be issued against him or her for contempt, or (conceivably) a bench warrant for his or her arrest may be issued, if he or she neglects to attend as commanded. The equivalent command to a defendant is a summons.

### *Subpoena duces tecum*

A court order specifying items that a witness or other party is to bring (*duces*) in hand (*tecum*) or suffer penalty (*sub poena*).

### Summons/Judicial Summons

A judicial summons is addressed to a defendant in a legal proceeding. Typically, the summons will announce to the person to whom it is directed that a legal proceeding has been started against that person, and that a file has been started in the court records. The summons announces a dated by which the defendant(s) must either appear in court, or respond in writing to the court or the opposing party or parties.

## Tort

A civil wrong (as opposed to a criminal wrong), which may be either intentional or accidental. If someone is driving and hits an unoccupied parked car, they commit a tort in that they have caused a wrong to another party which does not rise to the level of a crime. If they fail to stop at the scene of the accident, they also commit a *crime*, which is a criminal wrong in addition to, and separate from the tort.

## Tortfeasor

The title given to an actor who commits a tort.

## Under Seal

A procedure allowing sensitive or confidential information to be filed with a court without becoming a matter of public record. The court generally must give permission for the material to remain under seal.

**Uphold**

To maintain.

**Venue**

Neighourhood, neighbouring place; synonymous with place of trial. It refers to the possible or proper place(s) for trial of a suit, as among several places where jurisdiction could be established.

There will be a number of legal (court) documents that your attorney will file on your behalf during the course of the lawsuit. Some will be simple, some will be complicated and they may in response to Plaintiff's documents, but the content of them will be commons sense, but penned in a legal structure.

www.ingramcontent.com/pod-product-compliance
Lightning Source LLC
Chambersburg PA
CBHW051343170526
45166CB00002B/942